# THIS Book. IS @ gift

From

_______________________________

To

_______________________________

On the Occasion of

_______________________________

Date

_______________________________

**PUBLISHED IN NIGERIA BY:**
FREEDOM PUBLICATIONS
21, Adesuwa Grammar School Road, GRA.
P.O.BOX 7240, Benin City, Nigeria.
Tel: 08022908737, 08023381077
Email: bishopchigbundu@gmail.com
Website: www.voiceoffreedomministries.org

**DESIGN & PRINTS:**
Aaron & Hur Publishing *(A member of the BSA Group)*
16, Thomas Salako Street, Ogba-Ikeja, Lagos, Nigeria
Tel: 07035121346, 08097032664
Email: info@aaronandhurpublishing.com
W: www.aaronandhurpublishing.com

# CONTENTS

# Introduction

But upon mount Zion, there shall be deliverance, and there shall be holiness; and the house of Jacob shall possess their possession." Obadiah 1:17

Beloved, welcome to our Faith Clinic, Spiritual Hospital and Mount Zion, where Jesus is the Deliverer and Healer. My team and I are workers here and we follow the leading of the Holy Spirit who is The Director of Operations in the clinic. We promise we will give you every attention that will lead to your total and permanent deliverance.

Our goal is your total freedom and to this end, we have packaged some powerful prayer points on different areas to assist you obtain total freedom. In the manual, there are several investigations that will help you understand the root cause of your issues, and properly diagnose them for effective ministration. There are also principles laid down for you to follow to maintain your freedom.

Please, we would love you to use this booklet as a guide and prayer manual. We assure you that within    days of effectively going through these prayer points, God will give you the kind of deliverance you need with substantial evidence.

Beloved, we would want you to follow all instructions given in the Faith Clinic and attend all follow up ministrations to enable us deal with your issues thoroughly. Please note that there are twelve ministration follow up sessions you must undergo for effective and lasting results.

We are determined to see evidence in your life hence we will not let you go until that evidence appears. So give us the needed time for God to show up in your case.

All cases are not the same. Do not compare

yourself with someone else because you neither have the same destiny nor do you come from the same family. Some cases may require more time than others depending on the degree of the problem, the level of one's spiritual maturity and cooperation with God through the minister(s) handling their case.

We keep every information very confidential. Therefore, do not withhold any relevant information from our counselors. What you are hiding may be the opening through which the enemy entered into your life. It might be the key to the strong room of the enemy. Let us know what it is, no matter how private/personal it might seem to you. Please be open and sincere.

God is able to deliver you no matter the complexity of your case. He has delivered multitudes whose cases are similar or even worse than yours.

Dearly beloved, we want you to know that without you surrendering your life totally to Jesus, there is no amount of prayer that can guarantee your deliverance. Therefore, we implore you to surrender your whole life to

# DIAGNOSING YOUR SELF

# PART ONE

## PERSONAL PARTICULARS

We shall begin by examining certain basic information about you such as name, marital status, profession, age, position in your family, number of children, whether you are born again or not, etc.

## NAMES

A proper examination of the meaning of your name may give an idea of the spiritual problems in your life. Names have much spiritual significance thus they affect people either positively or negatively. Some great men in the Bible had their names changed so they could achieve God's purposes in their lives:

Abram to Abraham (Gen.17:5), Jacob to Israel (Gen.32:28), Simon to Peter (John 1:42), etc. Apart from those who actually effected a change of name, there are other evidences in scriptures to show that names do affect people. In

1Chronicles 4:9-10, Jabez found it necessary to pray away the negative influence of his sorrowful name before he could fulfill destiny, in 1Samuel 25:25, it took the intervention of Abigail to ward off the disaster that would have destroyed her entire household because of the foolish actions of her husband whose name "Nabal" not surprisingly, means "a fool". On the positive side, the name Joseph means "Addition or Adding" (Gen.30:24) - little wonder he was such a blessing to his family and generation. What is your name? Some names are tied to deities and other symbolic figures while others are given as a result of events that occurred before or during their birth.

There is a possibility that the person after whom you were named had an evil spirit controlling him so the same would be transferred to their namesakes.

## PROFESSION

Some professions easily expose one to demonic influences. Models, actors and actresses who act certain roles tend to be affected by those roles. They stand to be contaminated by the negative spirit responsible for certain evil characters which they (actors/actresses) portray when performing. Policemen who take bribes stand cursed, so also are doctors who specialize in abortions, judges who pervert judgment and preachers of the gospel who take God's glory.

## AGE & NUMBER OF CHILDREN

A married lady may be 36 years old with only one child and finds that she is not able to bear more children. This should prompt such a person to take a look at their family history with a view to finding out if this is a common phenomenon in the family. If the answer is yes, then there is something wrong.

A man who is 40 years old and says "I am not interested in marriage" whereas he has no gift of celibacy has every reason to examine himself critically. He may be married in the spirit realm. Also, where a person is grown in age and has all the relevant qualifications and experience and yet cannot make any headway in life despite all required efforts, it indicates that a spirit of setback is on assignment in his life. A thorough examination should be made to find out the basis of the operation of this spirit.

## POSITION IN FAMILY TREE

Firstborn children need to ask many questions about circumstances surrounding their conception and delivery. They are normally dedicated to the idols in the family or the family shrine. This is even more so when one's parents worship/worshipped idols.

If you are the only male or female child after other sisters or brothers have been born, endeavour to ask questions about how your mother gave birth to you. The same thing applies if you are the only child or an only surviving child.

Equally important are records of twins, who are believed in many places to possess certain powers because they are normally dedicated to spirits and sealed with a blood covenant. Do you find yourself in any of these? It's time to liberate yourself.

## BLOOD COVENANTS

Blood covenants are very strong because according to the Bible blood is the very life of a person or an animal (Lev. 17:11; Gen. 4:10). Generally, a covenant is a formal agreement made between two or more parties. The blood of Jesus offered on the cross, was to seal the covenant made by God with man so that man may receive the promise of an eternal inheritance. A blood covenant, therefore, is an agreement that is made between an individual or group of individuals on the one hand and a deity on the other; it is then sealed with blood. Hence, whenever rituals are performed and a human being or an animal is sacrificed, what it means is that whatever is the agreement between the idol and the people offering the sacrifice, has been sealed by the spilled blood of the person or animal as the case may be. (1Cor.10:20-22).

## ARE YOU BORN AGAIN?

This question is very important. It does not necessarily mean whether you are a member of a Christian church or not. The question seeks to know whether you have heard the gospel of Jesus Christ and come to the realization that you are a sinner and this realization prompted you to repent and confess your sins to Jesus Christ for forgiveness. If you are born again, do you have a testimony to give about your new birth and can you support your status with scriptures?

The reason this is so important is because only children of God are qualified to receive deliverance from the clutches of satan and his agents. John 1:12 says these are those who have believed in the name of Jesus and received the right/privilege to be so addressed. The fact that your name is in the register of a church does not make you a Christian at all. No. Should demons be cast out of you in this state, they would rush back to their dwelling positions because the Word of God, which is power and sword of the Spirit does not reside in you.

It is therefore of utmost importance that you pause at this point and pray in sincerity, this simple prayer of surrender to the Lordship of Jesus Christ: "Lord Jesus, I believe that You are the Son of God and I thank You for coming into this world and bearing my sins on Your own body on the cross. I know that I am a sinner and that I cannot save myself; therefore I put my trust in Your sacrifice for sin. I repent of all my sins, I confess and forsake them all. I renounce the devil and all his evil works, I open my heart and ask You to come in and become my Lord and personal Saviour. Right now, I believe that my sins are forgiven and my name written in the Book of Life. According to Your Word therefore, I receive the power to live as a child of God above sin, satan and the world. Thank You Jesus for what You have done for me. Amen." Praise God! If you prayed the above prayer from your heart, you are now born again and hence, qualified to receive deliverance from God.

## PRESENT COMPLAINTS AND DURATION

The purpose of this investigation is to ascertain whether you are suffering from any sickness that has defied medical solution. If this is so, then your problem requires spiritual attention.

In certain cases, the problem would not necessarily be sickness but marital, financial, lack of progress in life or various forms of relationship problems (frequent misunderstandings, hatred without cause, rejection, denial etc).

# PART TWO

# FAMILY SPIRITUAL EXPOSURE

Our foundation comes from our parents hence the need to know their spiritual background.

1. A parent who is not a born again Christian may have an idol which he serves to get protection.

2. If your parents worshiped or still worship idols, then you stand the danger of having been dedicated to the family god or shrine.

3. Because your parents worshipped or worship idols, you carry a curse. (Exodus 20:6; Deut. 27:15).

4. Where parents were or are polygamists, there is the likelihood that the same spirit would have transferred onto their offspring thereby causing all sorts of problems in their relationships in and outside of marriage.

5.  In a situation where ones parents or spouse have been involved in white garment churches i.e. Cherubim & Seraphim, Brotherhood of the Cross and Star, Celestial, Divine Healers, Holy Sabbath, etc, there is the danger of the transference of occult spirit, spirit of divination and religious spirit. Moreover, involvement (in) with syncretism predisposes one to spiritual defilement through the spirit of error in charge of such sects.

6. There is the possibility of the deity of a particular shrine marrying the women in the family. This can also bring about setbacks in the lives of the members of the family.

7.  In the case where your grandparents, uncles, etc were chiefs, priests/priestesses or queen mothers, there is a curse by way of idol worship and blood covenants through animal/human sacrifice.

8. It is a known fact that people in such profession as hunting acquire spiritual powers either for protection or to enable them to and game. This could result in a guardian spirit being assigned to the family in addition to being placed under a curse. Therefore, where ones parents and/or grandparents have been involved in this profession it would be wise for such a person to subject him/herself to deliverance ministrations.

9. What is the symbol of your clan? Is it a tiger, a lion, deer or any other animal? The Bible says "Do not become corrupt and make for yourselves an idol, an image of any shape, whether formed like a man or a woman, or like any animal on earth, or any bird that lies in the air or like any creature that moves along the ground, or any fish in the waters below. And when you look up to the sky and see the sun, the moon and the stars all the heavenly array do not be enticed into bowing down to them and worshipping things the Lord your God has apportioned to all the nations."(Deut. 4:16-19).

   The symbol of your clan is an identification of a given demon that guards the clan. By his position, he rules and influences the clan. In some cases, he marries the women in it and because the clan has chosen an image of an animal as an idol, contrary to the Word of God, that family unknowingly, brings itself under a curse.

10. Find out whether at any point in time, any member of your family was involved in slave trade or any form of human sacrifice for whatever reason.

# PART THREE

# PERSONAL SPIRITUAL EXPOSURE

In this section you are required to identify how, through ignorance, you may have personally invited demons into your life. Here, you have to take a retrospective look at your past involvements in places such as white or red garment churches, occult groups, shrines, native or witch doctors and whatever covenants and dedications you may have made. It is important for the purpose of prayers, to make a list of the shrines, rivers, burial grounds, evil forests or any other ungodly place you may have visited, including occult groups you may have been part of.

If your church is a white or red garment church then you stand to be contaminated by the following spirits:

* Religious spirits
* Water spirits
* Occult spirits
* Divination spirits
* Charismatic witchcraft spirits.

# EFFECTIVE DELIVERANCE PRAYERS

This is so because virtually all of such churches derive their powers from water spirits to perform their wonders. Think back to see whether you have participated in any sacrifice/ritual. If your findings are positive, you must note the nature of the sacrifice/ritual (1Cor.10:20-22).

Carefully examine yourself in the following areas:

1. Do you have any incisions? Find out what led to the incision i.e. for healing, power, good luck, good marriage, fruit of the womb, prosperity, protection, etc. Note that your blood is your life and so when you use it for any ritual, you have given out your life.

2. Dedication to family gods could be the foundation of demonic operations in your life. Find out the names of the family gods. This will facilitate deliverance when in prayer you specifically destroy the dedication and its influence and break any stronghold in your life.

3. Members of armed robbery groups, kidnap gangs, drug, gambling syndicates and secret cults on initiation are made to take oaths of secrecy. Indicate to which of the groups you belong(ed) so that the oath could be broken and the spirit commanded to leave.

4. (a) Participation in cultural dances and masquerades. Here, we are talking about such cultural dances that involve performance of any form of rituals before

commencing.
(b) Involvement in traditional/heathen festivals (1Cor 10:20-22)

5. Palm reading, white magic, horoscope/ astrology and fortune telling. Your participation in any of these would invite curses upon you and expose you to occult powers (Isaiah 47:11-14; Deut.18:10-12).

6. Involvement in transcendental meditation groups i.e. Eckankar, Grail Message, Yoga, Hari-krishna, Syncretism, make you contaminated by occult spirits and spirits of error. They also bring one under a curse.

7. Use of charms, blessed pictures of so-called spiritual leaders, incense, talisman, prayer candles, protection rings, rosary, special soaps and creams, sponge, handkerchiefs and Florida water. In each of these cases, the user is requesting for the protection of some other spirits apart from that of the Almighty God; and this practice both contaminates and brings one under a curse.

8. If any curse has been placed upon your family or on you by anybody living or dead at one time or the other, you have to find out so that it could be dealt with specifically. Find out if there is any misfortune being suffered by most members of the family.

9. If you have undergone a puberty rite or age grade initiation you may be contaminated by ancestral age-group spirits or witchcraft.

10. The reading of such mystic books like"Six and Seven Books of Moses, "Egyptian Book of the Dead", "The Wisdom of Solomon", any book authored by the late renowned mystic, D. Lawrence, etc., are sure to open doors in your life to occult spirits.

11. Indulgence in films/drama or reading novels that portray various dimensions of horror, pornography and violence makes one susceptible to spiritual defilement.

12. Female circumcision leads to blood covenant with the spirit of immorality and ancestral spirits.

# PART FOUR

# PERSONAL STRANGE PHENOMENA

**1. Hallucination** – Hallucinatory spirit, split personality, schizophrenia (mind controlling spirit), etc could result into complete madness.

**2. Dejavu** – The feeling of having experienced the present situation before. For instance, an event may happen in the present, and it would appear to you, as if you had experienced it previously. You may also sometimes get to a place and it would appear to you as if you have been there before, whereas in reality you have not. Familiar spirits are responsible for such occurrences.

**3. Clairvoyance** – This practice bestows on one the ability to see in one's mind either future events or things that are happening or existing out of sight. Most of the things seen happening are evil. You may, for instance, "see" that an accident is going to happen and it actually does occur. If you had this ability when you were an unbeliever and it continues after you have become a Christian, then it is possible that you may have been contaminated by the spirit of divination and prediction, which are gifts offered by marine/water spirits. This is very different from the gift which the Spirit of God gives to genuine believers which also manifests in the physical.

4. Do you have additional money or other items, which you do not know how they came about? In such a case, you may have one or more of the following spirits: marine, dwarf or  spirit husband/ wife.

5. Missing of personal effects, articles and money could be attributed to marine spirits, dwarfs or a curse in the family.

6. If you have worn a ring, clothes or bangles which you never knew how you got them, then water spirits, spirit wife or husband and dwarfs could be responsible.

7. Have you lost your engagement/wedding ring under strange/unclear circumstances? The cause could be a witchcraft attack or the attack could be from a spirit husband /wife or water spirit. Their purpose is to break the marriage.

8. Do you experience miscarriages, and at what months do they occur? Here, the problem could be attributed to:
   (i)  covenant of barrenness
   (ii)  spirit husband

(iii) witchcraft attack.
Take particular note of any specific thing(s) that usually happen(s) before the miscarriage occurs.

**9. Are you excessively stubborn?** Two spirits may be at work here:
    (i)  Water spirit
    (ii)  Witchcraft spirit

**10. Are you callous?** That is, do you enjoy seeing others suffer? Callousness is one of the characteristics of witchcraft.

**11. Are you restless?** Restlessness could be caused by either marine spirits or the spirit of insanity.

12. Are you addicted to alcohol, sex, music, sleep, tobacco, drug or food? Then you are likely to have a problem with the spirit of addiction. When it has to do with sleep, then the spirit of poverty is involved (Proverbs 6:10-11).

13. Terrible pains during menstrual period without any medical explanation might be due to deposits left in the womb during sex dreams.

**14. Are you lazy?** It could be the activity of a strong marine spirit. The affected person may be rich in the spirit realm and this "wealth" in the spirit realm subconsciously fills the victim with a false sense of contentment making them very unwilling to exert themselves in any work. Such a person's life in the physical is usually bedeviled by lack and poverty.

15. Experiencing continuous dizziness even after medical intervention might be attributable to the spirit of infirmity.

16. When you are unable to maintain any lasting relationship with the opposite sex, then you may be suffering from spiritual marriage covenant, or witches are responsible.

17. Are you unable to have normal birth and yet your situation defies all medical explanation? The cause may be due to witchcraft attack or a curse.

18. Unaccountable leanness in spite of heavy eating could be traced to witchcraft attack or a curse.

19. Are you proud? Two spirits might be responsible here:
   (i)  water
   (ii)  spirit of pride

20. Do you experience setbacks in your life pursuits? Witchcraft attack or a curse might be responsible. Find out about your family background to establish the likely cause.

21. Sadness and moodiness without cause are

attributable to marine/water spirits.

22. Are you easily irritated? It could be traceable to water spirits.

23. Are you afraid of mixing with people hence, you always want to be alone? The following spirits might be responsible:
(I) water
(ii) rejection
(iii) suicide or
(iv) spirit husband/ wife.

24. Have you disappointed someone before? The nature or extent of the disappointment may have resulted in a curse being placed on you.

25. Have you been disappointed before? The likely result is that you may have become bitter and unforgiving. This state of mind hinders ones blessings and opens doors to the spirit of rejection.

26. If you discuss with strange voices from within or without, then you are oppressed by any one of the following spirits:
(i)     Schizophrenia – mind controlling spirits;
(ii)     Insanity. Do you hear voices from within or from external but invisible source? Most times these voices tend to torment the hearer because the voice is sponsored by

the spirit of mockery.

27. Unnatural feeling of heat movement in the body could be caused either by marine/water spirit or a covenant of barrenness. In the case of women suffering from the covenant of barrenness, they may feel movements around the waist and the abdomen. In some cases, the feeling of the heat could be attributable to witchcraft or affliction spirits. In your dream, you could see yourself packing or carrying firewood.

28. The feeling of an invisible presence around you, especially when you are alone, might be the work of:
(i) familiar spirits (ancestral guardian spirit);
(ii) spirit husband/wife;
(iii) anti-christ spirit that may be abusing the Holy Ghost, God or Jesus Christ.

PART FIVE

# PERSONAL CHARACTERISTICS

This section is dedicated to carefully examining the behavioral traits of the person.

1. Excessive anger, bitterness, hatred and jealousy might mean that you are being controlled by the spirits of anger, hatred, bitterness and jealousy. In certain cases, they may provide a hint as to what other spirits are controlling your life taking into account information provided under other headings.

2. Excessive fear of river, snakes and heights are traceable to water spirits.

3. Excessive sexual urge or repressed sexual appetite might be the work of spirit husband/wife, or contamination from past sexual life.

4. Indiscriminate sexual habit in the present or past could lead to demonic contaminations because you

may not know what power any of your sex partners has/had.

5. If you had engaged in or are still engaged in acts of sexual perversion (i.e. masturbation, homosexuality, lesbianism, bestiality), a curse could be operating against you (Deut. 27:21; Romans 1:26 & 28). Also, a spirit is responsible for each perversion.

a. In a situation where you had engaged or are still engaged in incest, a curse could be operating against you (Deut.27:20-23).
b. If you find it difficult to forget your former sex partner, the implications listed below may have resulted from the union:
i. transference of demons and curses
ii. spiritual marriage
iii. deposits of spiritual sediments

*"Know ye not that he which is joined to an harlot is one body. For the two, saith He, shall be one flesh" 1Cor. 6:16-18.*

There is a soul tie that needs to be broken.
6. Do you feel rejected, inferior, insecure, self pity, depressed, confused or do you always feel like weeping? Either the spirit of rejection or water spirit is responsible.

7. Do you think of dying or committing suicide? If the answer is yes, then you are possibly being oppressed by the spirit of death or suicidal spirit.

8. If you worry unnecessarily over situations, then you may be under the control of the spirit of fear and insecurity.

9. Are you someone who habitually wants something and at the same time does not want it? It is an indication that you might be under the influence of the spirit of indecision.

# PART SIX

# PECULIAR DREAM STATE

We are not referring to dreams we have when we have over-eaten. The emphasis is on peculiar dreams, which are regular or occasional in line with any of the situations described below. It must be noted here that God does speak to His children in dreams (Numbers 12:6). Also, God could allow you to see the spirit world for the purpose of revealing the enemy's plans.

1. When you forget your dreams often, or think you do not dream at all, it might mean that witchcraft powers do not want you to know their line of action against you. This is witchcraft attack or blind witchcraft manifestation.

2. Are you pursued by masqueraders, mad men, animals or snakes in your dreams? A 'yes' answer might be an indication that your life is under attack by witches.

3. When you dream of falling from a cliff or high

mountain into a bottomless ditch or climbing a high hill, it is a sign that your life is possibly under witchcraft attack with a view to causing you setback.

4. When you experience any of the following in your dream, it indicates the presence of the spirit of setback, stagnancy and non-achievement:
   (i) You sit for an examination without getting the result
   (ii) You are always climbing a staircase without getting to the top.
   (iii) You find yourself in your secondary school uniform/ dormitory
   (iv) You see yourself wandering in the forest.

5. Where you dream of attending regular meetings or going to specific markets, it is an indication that you are a victim of blind witchcraft.

6. The following dreams show the possibility that your life is under witchcraft attack:
   (i) Being strangled/shot
   (ii) Being pressed down while asleep
   (iii) Fighting with wild animals and human beings
   (iv) An attack which manifests physically.

7. When you wake up from your sleep with marks or cuts on your body, this could be an evidence of witchcraft attack on your life. These witches might

have taken your blood as a point of contact against you.

8.  When in your dreams you:
    (i) receive gifts, which sometimes manifest physically - this could be the work of spirit husband/wife or water spirit.
    (ii) Play with snakes – this is serpentine spirit.

9.  When you have any of the following dreams, it is an indication that the person is spiritually married:
    (i) Attending marriages or getting married.
    (ii) Sexual intercourse

10. A covenant of barrenness might be in force should you see yourself in any of the listed situations whether constantly or periodically in a dream:
    (i) pregnant, carrying babies or breast feeding babies.
    (ii) having sexual intercourse, seeing any of the following before your menstrual period: blood-stained sanitary pad, ripe fruits, red oil, fresh meat with blood

11. Swimming or playing with age-mates, standing at the bank of a river, crossing a river with a canoe or a boat all suggest that you are under the influence of a marine/water spirit.

12. How often do you eat in your dreams? This could be

an indication of witchcraft spirit, or it may mean the deposition of spiritual sediments in your body by witches.

13. Discussing or eating with dead relatives traces its source possibly to the spirit of death.

# 2

# CONFESSIONAL DELIVERANCE WARFARE PRAYER SECTION

*Friend, now that you have discovered what is wrong with you, I would like you to pray the following*

# PART ONE

# BREAKING OF EVIL ALTARS

1. Altars by the gate of my village, break by fire in Jesus' name.

2. Altars by our village shrine, scatter by fire in Jesus' name.

3. Altars connected to trees in my village, catch fire in Jesus' name.

4. Altars connected to the rivers and lakes in my village, break in Jesus' name.

5. Altars on my family shrine, break in the mighty name of Jesus.

6. Altars connected to my umbilical cord, be consumed by fire in Jesus' name.

7. Altars connected to my name, catch fire in Jesus'

mighty name.

8.  Altars that forbid consistent progress in my family, catch fire in Jesus' name.

9.  Altars against the progress of first sons and daughters, break by fire in Jesus' mighty name.

10. Altars against financial progress of first sons and daughters scatter by fire in the mighty name of Jesus.

11. Altars against the marriages of first sons and daughters, scatter by fire, in the mighty name of Jesus.

12. Altars against the progress of last sons and daughters, be destroyed by fire in the name of Jesus.

13. Altars connected to my blood line (father/ mother), I break your dominion over my life in Jesus' name.

14. Altars of stagnancy, I break you by the fire of the Holy Ghost in the name of Jesus.

15. Altars connected to the moon, I scatter your influence over my life by the fire of the Holy Ghost in Jesus' name.

16. Altars connected to the stars over my destiny, receive

fire in Jesus' name.

17. Altars connected to the sun controlling my destiny, scatter by fire in Jesus' name.

18. Altars connected to the wind to distract my destiny helpers from locating me, scatter by the fire of the Holy Ghost in Jesus' name.

19. Altars connected to rocks and stones, break by fire in Jesus mighty name.

20. Altars connected to evil birds speaking against my life, break in the mighty name of Jesus.

21. Altars connected to evil animals, scatter by fire in Jesus' name.

22. Altars connected to the food my tribe forbids, break in Jesus' name.

23. Altars connected to demonic cultural rites and practices in my village working against my life, scatter in Jesus' name.

24. Altars sponsoring financial limitation in my life, break in Jesus' name.

25. Altars sponsoring failure in my life, I break you by

fire in Jesus' name.

26. Altars sponsoring limitation in my life endeavors, catch fire in Jesus' mighty name.

27. Altars sponsoring business losses, catch fire in Jesus' mighty name.

28. Altars sponsoring business stagnation, expire by the fire of the Holy Ghost in Jesus' name.

29. Altars sponsoring evil pattern in my family, scatter by fire in the mighty name of Jesus.

30. Altars sponsoring patterns of untimely death in my family, break in the name of Jesus.

31. Altars sponsoring untimely death of the progressive sons and daughters of my family, I destroy you by thunder in Jesus' name.

32. Altars sponsoring patterns of sickness in my family, I break you by fire in Jesus' name.

33. Altars sponsoring poverty at old age, receive fire in Jesus' name.

34. Altars sponsoring late marriages in my family, break by fire in Jesus' name.

35. Altars sponsoring chronic singlehood in my family, catch fire now in the powerful name of Jesus.

36. Altars sponsoring death of intelligent children in my family, scatter by Holy Ghost fire in the mighty name of Jesus.

37. Altars sponsoring evil veil over my star, break by fire in Jesus' name.

38. Altars sponsoring blackmails against me, catch fire in Jesus' name.

39. Altars sponsoring forgetfulness in the hearts of my helpers, catch fire in Jesus' name.

40. Altars of disharmony and confusion in my family, break in Jesus' name.

41. Altars that destroy good opportunities that are coming to me, break by fire in Jesus' name.

42. Altars raised on the day I was born, break by fire in Jesus' name.

43. Altars connected to the market day I was born, the thunder of God locate and break you now in Jesus' mighty name.

44. Altars that scatter the labour of my hands, expire by the fire of the Holy Ghost in Jesus' name.

45. Altars sponsoring struggle and hardship in life, break by thunder in Jesus' name.

46. Altars from the places I went to for help hindering my progress in life, receive fire now in Jesus' mighty name.

47. Altars raised through sexual immoralities hindering my marital settlement and progress, break in Jesus' name.

48. Altars raised through circumcision, expire in Jesus' name.

49. Altars established through sacrifices at various junction, receive fire in Jesus' name.

50. Altars in the street where I live, break in Jesus' name.

51. Altars in the place where I work, scatter by fire in Jesus' name.

52. Altars in the place where I do my business expire, in Jesus' name.

53. Altars in the city, town or village where I live break in

Jesus' name.

54. Altars connected to snakes, catch fire in Jesus' mighty name.

55. Altars connected to the totem of my village/ family, scatter by fire in Jesus' mighty name.

56. Altars that limit educational lifting in my life catch fire now, in Jesus' name.

57. Altars that limit professional lifting in my life break from my life in Jesus' name.

58. Altars that limit my spiritual lifting, scatter by fire in Jesus' name.

59. Altars sponsoring quarrel and confusion in my marriage, catch fire in Jesus' name.

60. Altars sponsoring sickness in my body, scatter by fire in Jesus' name.

61. Altars raised with my hair and finger nails, break in Jesus' name.

62. Altars raised with my blood, scatter in Jesus' powerful name.

63. Altars with ancient money like cowries and manilas representing my money, catch fire in Jesus' name.

64. Altars raised by native doctors with salt against my destiny, scatter by fire in Jesus' name.

65. Altars raised by native doctors with sand against me, scatter by fire in Jesus' name.

66. Altars raised by native doctors with my picture, catch fire in the mighty name of Jesus.

67. Altars raised by native doctors with snail and tortoise to slow down progress in my life, scatter by thunder in Jesus' name.

68. Altars raised against me by native doctors with powder and native chalk, scatter by fire in Jesus' name.

69. Altars raised by occult power using enchantment and curses against me, break in Jesus' name.

70. Altars of Ogun, Eziza, Olokun, Orunmila, Sango, Amadioha, Ahanjoku, Igbe, (mention the gods in your community) scatter by the Holy Ghost fire in Jesus' name.

71. Altars of servitude in my family/village, break in Jesus'

name.

72. By the anointing of the Holy Ghost, I deploy the blood of Jesus against representatives of evil altars in my life. I command them to come out by air or liquid through my mouth and other openings of my body, in Jesus' mighty name.

## PART TWO

# SILENCING THE VOICE OF EVIL SACRIFICES

1.  Evil sacrifices speaking against my destiny, be silent forever in Jesus' name.

2.  I silence the voice of evil sacrifices speaking failure into my life in Jesus' name.

3.  By the power in the blood of Jesus, I silence the voices of evil sacrifices speaking sickness into my body in Jesus' mighty name.

4.  You voice of evil sacrifices speaking limitations into my life, be silent in Jesus' name.

5.  By thunder and fire, I destroy the power of evil sacrifices speaking disapproval in the hearts of my destiny helpers in Jesus' name.

6.  Evil sacrifices speaking delays in my life, be silent forever in Jesus' name.

7. I deploy the power in the blood of Jesus to silence the voice of evil sacrifices speaking stagnancy into my life in Jesus' name.

8. Evil sacrifices speaking poverty into my life be silent forever in Jesus' name.

9. I silence the voice of evil sacrifices speaking hardship and struggle into my life in Jesus' name.

10. By the power in the blood of Jesus, I silence the voice of evil sacrifices speaking financial hardship and limitation into my life in Jesus' name.

11. I destroy the voices of evil sacrifices speaking failure and stagnation into my business in Jesus' name.

12. I silence the voices of evil sacrifices speaking against my academic and professional progress in Jesus' name.

13. You evil voice from strong sacrifices speaking against my marriage and home be silenced forever in Jesus' mighty name.

14. Evil sacrifices speaking against my ministry, church growth and expansion, be silent forever in Jesus' name.

15. I deploy the blood of Jesus against every evil sacrifices

speaking against my progress, greatness and lifting in Jesus' name.

16. You wicked voices from my family altar, speak no more in Jesus' name.

17. You wicked voice from my father's altars, be silent forever in Jesus' name.

18. You strange voice from my mother's altars speak no more in Jesus' name.

19. You evil voice speaking from my village altars against my destiny, be silent forever in Jesus' name.

20. All deposits representing voices from wicked altars, I command you to come out of me by air or liquid through my mouth and nose in Jesus' name.

## PART THREE

# HOW TO DEAL WITH ANCESTRAL SPIRITS AND COVENANTS

1. In the name of Jesus, by the anointing of the Holy Ghost and by my will, I break every covenant made by my ancestors to the ruling powers in my village and family.

2. In the name of Jesus, by the anointing of the Holy Ghost, and by my own will, I destroy every dedication to ancestral spirits by my ancestors.

3. I break all links and connections to the ancestral spirits in Jesus' name.

4. I destroy the dominion, protection and lordship of ancestral spirits over my life in the name of Jesus.

5. In the name of Jesus, I transfer out of my life every spirit of polygamy, divorce, marriage instability through my parents.

6. Every financial, marital, physical and health problems transferred into me through the blood line, I destroy and command you to come out of me now in Jesus' name.

7. You spirit assigned to monitor and hinder the progress of sons and daughters in my family, I terminate your assignment in my life today in the name of Jesus.

8. You evil monitoring spirit I command you to loose your hold from my life, pack your point of contact and go in Jesus' name.

9. You spirit assigned against marriages in my family, I terminate your assignment in my marriage in the name of Jesus.

10. You spirit in charge of untimely death in my family, I terminate your assignment in my life and I command you to loose your hold from my life pack your deposits and go in Jesus' name. I refuse to die like my ancestors in Jesus' name.

11. I break every link with the ancestral spirit which was established with my placenta and umbilical cord in Jesus' name.

12. In the name of Jesus, I wipe out my names from the spiritual family register with the blood of Jesus.

13. I cut off my branch from the tree of poverty in my family in Jesus' name.

14. I cut off my branch from every tree of adversity in my family in the mighty name of Jesus.

15. In the name of Jesus, I redeem my life from every curse running in my family.

16. In the name of Jesus, I revoke the curses through idol worship in my family.

17. I terminate the assignments of evil spirits operating in my family as a result of these curses in Jesus' name.

18. In the name of Jesus, I terminate the assignment of wicked spirits trailing me because of my family name.

19. You spirit of non-achievement and setback operating in my family, I destroy your power and infuuences in my life in the name of Jesus. I command you to pack your properties from my life and go in Jesus' name.

20. You family controller spirit assigned to operate at a certain age in my life I terminate your assignment and I command the Holy Ghost fire to consume your timetable in my life in Jesus' name.

21. Every blood covenant that was entered into by my

ancestors through sacrifices and pouring of libation, I nullify all with the blood of Jesus, in the name of Jesus.

22. In the name of Jesus, I destroy every wrong foundation laid by my ancestors, and I lay a new foundation with the blood of Jesus.

23. In the name of Jesus, I destroy all evil altars in my father's house and I lay a new altar with the blood of Jesus.

24. All covenants entered into by my parents on my behalf which now affects me, I destroy all in Jesus' name.

25. Every spirit operating in any area of my life as a result of such covenants I destroy your power, I bind you now and I command you to loose your hold from my life and go in Jesus' name.

26. I take authority and overthrow the reign and dominion of the strongman in my family in Jesus' name.

27. Now, all representatives, points of contact and deposits of the ancestral spirit and family controller spirits, I command all of you to come out of me now in Jesus' name.

# PART FOUR

# HOW TO RELEASE YOURSELF FROM EVERY CURSE

1. In the name of Jesus, I break and revoke every curse operating in my family.

2. In the name of Jesus, I break and revoke any curse of poverty, barrenness, non-achievement, setback, unfruitfulness and untimely death which may be on either or both sides of my  family back to four generations.

3. I command every evil power of these curses to release me and go out of me now in Jesus' name.

4. I revoke curses pronounced by witches and witch doctors against me in Jesus' name.

5. I revoke curses upon my life as a result of my wicked activities in the past in Jesus' name.

6. I revoke curses upon me as a result of my immoral life

with the married in Jesus' name.

7. I revoke curses upon me as a result of cheating the widow and the orphan in Jesus' name.

8. I revoke curses upon my life as a result of abortion(s) I committed or assisted someone to commit in Jesus' name.

9. I revoke curses upon me because of my involvement with native doctors, occult groups and witch doctors in Jesus' name.

10. I revoke curses upon me as a result of worshipping other gods in Jesus' name.

11. I command all spirits in my life as a result of the above curses to loose their hold in my life, pack their points of contact and go in Jesus' name.

12. In the name of Jesus, I command everything that represents curses in my life to come out of me now in Jesus' name.

13. I break every curse of failure and I bind the spirit in charge of near - success syndrome in my life in Jesus' name.

14. Every door of blessing, success, favour and

breakthrough closed by the spirits behind these curses, I command you now, open in Jesus' name.

15. I release and receive all my blessings that were delayed in Jesus' name.

16. All spirits, deposits and points of contact of curses, pack your load and come out of me right now in Jesus' name.

17. I erase all evil marks of curses in my life in Jesus' name. I establish new marks of favour and blessings in my life from today in Jesus' name.

18. I revoke every curse pronounced upon me by my parents in Jesus' name.

19. You spirits operating on parental curses in my life, I bind you and command you to lose your hold from my life, pack your points of contact and go in Jesus' name.

# PART FIVE

# HOW TO BREAK SPIRITUAL MARRIAGE COVENANTS

1. In the name of Jesus, by the power of the Holy Ghost and by my own will, I break the covenant of spiritual marriage in my life.

2. Any covenant of marriage to family deities or ancestral spirits by my parents or ancestors before or after I was born or after by my ancestors, I break it in the name of Jesus.

3. Any spiritual covenant of marriage established by me through sexual immorality with an agent of the devil, I break it in the name of Jesus.

4. Any spiritual covenant of marriage through association, involvement with native/witch doctors, the occult, demonic prayer houses, spiritualists, I break it in the name of Jesus.

5. In the name of Jesus, by the power of the Holy Ghost

and by my own will, I divorce you spiritual marriage partner.

6. In the name of Jesus, I command everything that entered into me through sexual dreams to come out of me now.

7. In the name of Jesus, I command every representative and point of contact of the spiritual partner to come out of me now.

8. In the name of Jesus, I release myself from every curse meant to hinder me from getting married in the physical.

9. Every curse by the spiritual partner that I will not have any physical child, I revoke it now in Jesus' name.

10. I release my marriage from every ancestral curse in Jesus' name.

11. I release my marriage from anti-marriage spirit assigned against sons and daughters in my family in Jesus' name.

12. I revoke and break all marital curses placed on me by my family's enemies in Jesus' name.

13. Every witchcraft spirit assigned to hinder me from

getting married, I bind you and command you to loose your hold from my marriage in Jesus' name.

14. You spirit responsible for marriage disappointment, I bind you and command you to loose your hold from my marriage in Jesus' name.

15. Anything in me that makes prospective life partners to run from me I destroy you and command you to come out of me now in Jesus' name.

16. Anything in my life that attracts the wrong prospective life partners to me, I destroy you now in Jesus' name.

17. You family deities from both sides of my parents holding me from getting married, release me and my marital life in Jesus' name.

18. In the name of Jesus, from today, I refuse to follow the evil pattern of late or failed marriages in my family.

19. In the name of Jesus, I release myself from every curse not to get married by my former boy or girl friend.

20. In the name of Jesus, I command Holy Ghost fire to consume anything that represents me in the coven of witches.

21. My life partner, I release you from every evil power that has hindered you from locating me in Jesus' name.

22. Lord, release my life partner to me, in Jesus' name.

23. My life partner, hear my voice wherever you are and come to me in Jesus' name.

24. My life partner, I release you from the spirit of indecision in Jesus' name.

25. Dear Holy Ghost, help me to locate and know my life partner in Jesus' name.

26. In the name of Jesus, I will get married to the right partner this year.

27. I release all resources I would need for my marriage in the name of Jesus.

## PART SIX

---

# CONFESSIONAL/DELIVERANCE PRAYERS FOR FRUIT OF THE WOMB

1.  Gen 1:28a: My Father in heaven, Your Word is true. I claim the promise and I confess that I am fruitful and multiplying. This promise shall be fulfilled in my life in Jesus' name.

2.  Every power that has hindered my fruitfulness, I command you to be destroyed in Jesus' name.

3.  Ex. 23:25-26: I serve the Lord God of heaven, therefore, my bread and water are blessed. He has taken away sickness from me and I will not miscarry any of my children.

4.  The Lord has spoken that none shall be barren among His children. Therefore, I confess that I am not and I cannot be barren in Jesus' name. Luke 1:45.

5.  Any authority and satanic conspiracy manipulating my reproductive organs into barrenness, I command

you to loose your hold now, in Jesus' name.

6.  Duet. 7:14: I confess that I am blessed above all people. Jehovah, who cannot lie, has spoken that there shall not be male or female barren among His children. Father I am your child; therefore, this promise shall be ful lled in my life.

7. I refuse bind and reject every spirit of barrenness, in Jesus' name.

8.  I destroy every program of satan to make me barren in Jesus' name.

10. I will be a mother of children, in Jesus' name. (Psalms113:9)

11. Psalms 127:3: Oh, Lord, give me my heritage. Give my womb a reward.

12. Children, I call you to come because you are God's heritage to me.

13. Every satanic hand against my ability to have children, I command you wither and be destroyed in Jesus' name.

14. Every witchcraft seed inside my reproductive organs meant to hinder me from becoming pregnant, I crush

you, come out of me now in Jesus' name. Mtt.15:13.

15. You witchcraft manipulation against my menstrual cycle, be destroyed, in Jesus' name.

16. Satanic heat in my womb and waist, I command you to vanish in Jesus' name.

17. You witchcraft spirit in charge of barrenness, in the name of Jesus, loose your hold from my reproductive organs and come out of me.

18. Witchcraft spirit assigned to prevent pregnancy in my life, I terminate your assignment in Jesus' name.

19. Witchcraft spirit assigned against my sperm count, I terminate your assignment now in Jesus' name.

20. Satanic powers on assignment against my reproductive organ, in the name of Jesus, I terminate your assignment and I release my organ from your control.

21. You demonic powers responsible for impotency and weakness of my male organ, loose your hold from my male organ now in Jesus' name.

22. You spirit in charge of watery sperm, I command Holy Ghost fire to consume you now in Jesus' name.

23. You spirits from my family that have vowed to hinder me from having children, I bind you now and I command you to loose your hold from my life and go in Jesus' name.

24 Every witchcraft spirit responsible for miscarriage of pregnancies in my life, be destroyed now in Jesus' name.

25. I wipe off my names from the satanic register of childless couples in Jesus' name.

26. You spiritual partner, I hate you. I don't want you again in my life. Be gone forever in Jesus' name.

27. Every link between me and any spiritual partner is hereby broken, in Jesus' name.

28. Everything that was transferred from you to me during sexual dreams, I command them to be flushed out of me now in Jesus' name.

29. By my will and in the name of Jesus, I tear the marriage certificate into pieces. I command the Holy Ghost Fire to consume the wedding ring now in Jesus' name.

30. In the name of Jesus, I declare openly today that I am no more married to you and your dominion and

influence over me is hereby destroyed in Jesus' name.

31. Every curse from spiritual partner that I will not have any physical children is hereby destroyed. I reverse the curse in Jesus' name.

32. I confess that I will have as many children as I want in the physical in Jesus' name.

33. In the name of Jesus, I disown every spiritual child in the realm of the spirit.

34. Every object that moves around my reproductive organ, I command you, be destroyed and come out of me in Jesus' name.

35 In Jesus' name, I flush out every witchcraft point of contact in my reproductive system with the blood of Jesus.

36. Every witchcraft point of contact through food and drink in the dream, be flushed out of me now in Jesus' name.

37. I revoke every witchcraft curse of barrenness in my life in Jesus' name.

38. I revoke every curse on me as a result of abortions I committed in the past in Jesus' name.

39. Every curse pronounced against me by a former partner to hinder me from having babies, I revoke it now in Jesus' name.

40. I release myself from the consequences of such curses and command every representative to come out of me now in Jesus' name.

41. I refuse to remain under any curse as a result of my family or spouse's background in Jesus' name.

42. I refuse to remain under any covenant made by any of my ancestors in Jesus' name.

43. Ancestral spirits in my family and village, (mention their names) hear my voice now: In the name of Jesus, I break every link between us. From today, you shall have no in uence or dominion over my life in Jesus' name.

44. Every concoction I drank, every charm I made and every involvement with spiritualists which now hinders me from having babies, I destroy all in Jesus' name.

45. In the name of Jesus, I release my life, reproductive organs and my children from every power that operates in the\ air, water, sun, moon, stars, forests, stones and ground.

46. In the name of Jesus and with the blood of Jesus, I wipe out every hand writing of childlessness written against me.

47. My marriage, I deliver you from the spirits of childlessness.

48. I refuse to be childless. I shall deliver my own children, in Jesus' name.

49. My babies, I release you from wherever you have been held captive and I command you to come to me now in the name of Jesus.

50. My womb, male organ, I release you from wherever you are tied in Jesus' name.

51. Witchcraft spirits, leave me alone in Jesus' name.

52. Water spirits, you are not the giver of children. I denounce you and I break every covenant with you, in Jesus' name.

53. Spirits from the water, leave me alone. I don't belong to you anymore in Jesus' name (Shout it).

54. You spirit against child-bearing in my family, in the name of Jesus, I destroy your power over my life. Release your hold and get out of my life.

55. Every witchcraft hand holding my reproductive system, I command you to be paralyzed now, in Jesus' name.

56. I decree death on every witch responsible for my childlessness, in the name of Jesus.

57. I shall have my babies. I decree and declare that this month is my month of fruitfulness. Childlessness has expired in my life in Jesus' name.

58. In the name of Jesus, I disown all spirit children hindering me from having my physical children.

59. In the name of Jesus, I destroy every child representing my children in the realms of the spirit.

60. In the name of Jesus, I destroy the spiritual home interfering with my physical home, in Jesus' name.

61. You spiritual home, children and partner, I command the fire of the Holy Ghost to consume you now in Jesus' name.

62. From today, I am free from your harassments, in Jesus' name. Every strange heat in my reproductive organs I command you to stop in Jesus' mighty name.

63. My womb receive my husband's seed, fertilize it and

let healthy babies be formed now in Jesus name.

64. My sperm receive life and produce babies in Jesus' name.

65. My womb, you will not miscarry this baby in Jesus' mighty name.

66. No baby will die in my womb in Jesus' name.

67. No fruit of my womb shall be deformed or malformed, in Jesus' name.

68. My pregnancy shall be trouble free, in Jesus' name.

69. In the name of Jesus, I shall have quick and complication free labour and safe delivery.

70. I shall not die with this pregnancy in Jesus' name.

# PART SEVEN

# HOW TO DESTROY WITCHCRAFT SPIRITS' ACTIVITIES, MANIPULATIONS AND DEPOSITS

1. Father, in the name of Jesus Christ, Your only begotten Son, I take my place in Your kingdom. I ask for and receive the anointing that destroys the power and influence of witches and wizards.

2. Standing on the Word of God in Galatians 3:13, I revoke every witchcraft curse. I bind the spirits that gained access into my life through witchcraft curses.

3. I bind and cast out every spirit that has brought disfavour, disappointments, sickness and inability to marry etc. into my life.

4. I remove every protection enjoyed by the witches and wizards and I break off their legs from that circle of protection.

5. I destroy the witchcraft altar in my life; I vandalize their altar with the blood of Jesus.

6.  I disconnect every witchcraft point of contact in my life in the name of Jesus.

7.  Witchcraft spirits, whatever is your legal ground, I nullify it with the blood of Jesus Christ.

8. I release the Holy Ghost fire to the genesis of the witchcraft attack and activities on my life, marriage, finances, business, health, e.t.c.

9.  I wipe out any witchcraft mark on my fore-head or any part of my body through which they are able to trace me wherever I go (I King 21:8-9) in the mighty name of Jesus.

10. I bind the highest authority of the witches' coven where my case is tabled. I destroy your power and your seat of leadership. I blind your eyes towards me with the Holy Ghost fire in the name of Jesus.

11. In the name of Jesus, I bind the executive members of the coven where my case is being tabled. Let there be misunderstanding and trouble between them. I decree that whatever they have planned against my life be scattered now.

12) In the name of Jesus, I bind the witches and wizards whether they be physical or spiritual who reported or took my case to the coven. I discharge myself from their accusations. According to the Word of God in

Psalm 112:10, I command their desire against me to perish in Jesus' name.

13. I stand upon Matthew 16:19, I declare that the keys of the kingdom of heaven have been given to me therefore whatsoever I bind is bound and whatsoever I loose is loosed in heaven and on earth. Therefore, I stand against all evil messengers from whichever coven assigned to bring their evil plans against me to pass. I bind them, I frustrate their devices and lock all doors against them in the name of Jesus.

14. I command the fire of the Holy Ghost to consume the witches and wizards working against me, in Jesus' name.

15. In the name of Jesus, I refuse to honour any evil physical or spiritual invitations or summons.

16. In the name of Jesus I reject any honour, favour or promotion projected from the coven to set me up and destroy me. I nullify these plans; they will not work, in the name of Jesus.

17. Job 22:28 says that, whatsoever I decree on earth shall be established in heaven. I now decree that every accusation in the coven against me be rendered null and void in the name of Jesus.

18. I discharge myself from every coven court. In the name of the greatest Judge, Jesus Christ of Nazareth, I am free! I am free indeed!

19. Oh Lord, in the name of Jesus Christ, I pull down completely the coven from where witches and wizards attack me.

20. I destroy every coven that has operated against me and decree in the name of Jesus that from today, it will no longer function; when they try to come together, it shall never work in Jesus' name.

21. In the name of Jesus and with the fire of the Holy Ghost, I destroy every witchcraft cage holding my womb.

22. In the name of Jesus, I destroy every witchcraft cage holding my business name, complimentary card, letter heads, etc.

23. In the name of Jesus, I tear and burn down every witchcraft blanket covering my business signboard.

24. Every witchcraft gates, barricades and checkpoints, I command you to be dismantled and be totally destroyed, in Jesus' name.

25. In the name of Jesus, you witchcraft chains of

stagnancy holding me to one spot, be destroyed now.

26. You witchcraft money introduced into my business, I command you to be destroyed now by the Holy Ghost fire in the mighty name of Jesus Christ.

27. Every witchcraft dominion over my life as a result of my past encounter with any witch doctor, I command you to be destroyed in the name of Jesus.

28. Any witchcraft altar raised against my business, health, academics etc, be destroyed now in the name of Jesus.

29. You witchcraft cobwebs that come upon me, be destroyed by fire in Jesus' name.

30. In the name of Jesus, I destroy every witchcraft burial done to project death into my life.

31. In the name of Jesus, I destroy, dismantle and scatter every witchcraft summon extended to me to manipulate me to submission.

32. I discharge and acquit myself from every witchcraft court. I destroy all the case files against me in the witchcraft court in the name of Jesus.

33. You evil lawyer handling my case in the coven, I make

my case to be too hot for you to handle, therefore, I command you to fall down and die in the name of Jesus.

34. In the name of Jesus, I expel from my body every witchcraft deposit through gun shot in the dream.

35. In the name of Jesus, I expel from my body every witchcraft deposit through injection in the dream.

36. In the name of Jesus I expel from my body every witchcraft deposit through drugs (tablets) in the dream.

37. I expel every witchcraft deposit through flogging in the dream in the name of Jesus

38. I cut off every witchcraft hand manipulating me to troubled places and disappointments in the dream.

39. Every witchcraft family altars in my life, be destroyed now in the name of Jesus.

40. You witchcraft strong man in my family, be destroyed in the name of Jesus.

41. Every witchcraft covering cast over my blessings, melt away in the name of Jesus.

42. In the name of Jesus, I overthrow every witchcraft kingdom in my family.

43. In the name of Jesus, I release my life from the dominion of witchcraft.

44. In the name of Jesus, I destroy every witchcraft pot of enchantment used against me and my family.

45. Witchcraft hand feeding me in the dream, be paralyzed right now, in the name of Jesus.

46. I destroy every witchcraft kitchen where evil food is being prepared for me in the name of Jesus.

47. In the name of Jesus, I destroy every witchcraft covering over my destiny.

48. In Jesus' name, I expel every witchcraft deposits through incisions on my body.

49. In Jesus' name, I expel from my body every witchcraft deposit through food in the dream.

50. I expel from my body every witchcraft deposit through sex in the dream in the name of Jesus.

51. In the name of Jesus, I destroy every witchcraft hand manipulating my reproductive system (womb, tube, sex organ, etc.)

52. Every witchcraft tree carrying the fruit of my womb, dry up and be burnt by fire in the name of Jesus.

53. In the name of Jesus, I burn every witchcraft tree carrying the fruit of the labour of my hands.

54. By the blood of Jesus, I wash away every disappointment spread over me by witches in Jesus' name.

55. By the blood of Jesus, I wash away every mark of failure and setback put upon my life from the coven in Jesus' name.

56. By the blood of Jesus, I wash away every mark put upon me by witches and wizards to manipulate my finances in the name of Jesus.

57. Any aspect of my character under witchcraft influence or manipulation be destroyed in Jesus' name.

58. In the name of Jesus, I destroy every witchcraft budget made for me and my family.

59. In the name of Jesus, I destroy every witchcraft controlled desires in my life.

60. In the name of Jesus, every witchcraft incantation and divination against my life, be revoked and be

destroyed.

61. Every witch and wizard using the weapon of dust against my life, fall down and die in Jesus' name.

62. I expel every spirit of sluggishness introduced into my life by witchcraft powers in Jesus' name.

63. In the name of Jesus, I destroy and expel every witchcraft-induced sickness in my life.

64. In the name of Jesus, I destroy every witchcraft prison where my destiny is locked up.

65. Lord, from today onwards, make my life a no-go-area for witches and wizards in Jesus' name.

66. In the name of Jesus and by the power in the blood of Jesus Christ, I break every witchcraft covenant and initiation in my life.

67. In the name of Jesus Christ, I destroy completely, all deposits of witchcraft initiation in my body. I   ush them out of my body in Jesus' name.

68. In the mighty name of Jesus Christ and by the power in His blood, I pull down every witchcraft stronghold in my life and I bind every strongman behind these strongholds in Jesus' name.

69. By the power in the blood of Jesus, I break any witchcraft covenant entered against me by my ancestors in my family in Jesus' name.

70. You witchcraft dominion over my life, I destroy you totally, in the mighty name of Jesus Christ.

71. I release myself and all my blessings from witchcraft dominion in Jesus' name.

72. In the name of Jesus Christ, I command the Holy Ghost fire to destroy all witchcraft monitoring gadgets projected at me.

73. You witchcraft spirits assigned to monitor my progress, family, business, academics and finances, be destroyed by fire in the name of Jesus.

74. By the power in the blood of Jesus Christ, I blot out from my family background every witchcraft handwriting of ordinances working against me in the name of Jesus Christ.

75. In the name of Jesus Christ, I reverse the evil witchcraft times and seasons set up in my family to negatively affect the labour of my family members.

76. I bind you witches and wizards assigned to enforce the wicked times and seasons in my life, in the name

of Jesus' name. I command you to be destroyed .

77. In the name of Jesus Christ, I reverse these wicked times and seasons to good times and seasons of divine favour in my life.

78. In the name of Jesus Christ and by the fire of the Holy Ghost, I raze down every witchcraft altar erected against me.

79. In the name of Jesus Christ and by the fire of the Holy Ghost, I raze down every witchcraft foundation in my life.

80. I command all witches and wizards assigned to minister against me from the altars of darkness to be consumed by the fire of the Holy Ghost in the name of Jesus Christ.

81. In the name of Jesus Christ, I utterly condemn every witchcraft counsel taken against me.

82. You hands of wickedness that have banded yourselves together against me, I destroy your plans and put confusion in your midst in Jesus' name.

83. You witchcraft power blocking my blessings from the four corners of the earth, Be consumed by fire in Jesus' name.

84. Every witchcraft power speaking against me, I command you to be silent now in Jesus' name ( I Sam. 2:9).

85. I command the dwelling places of witchcraft to be desolate in Jesus' name. (Job 8:22)

86. O you heavens, rain snares fire and brimstone on the witches and wizards that are depriving me access to my opportunities in Jesus' name. (Psalm 11:6).

87. You witchcraft spirits, by the authority of the eternal Word of God in Isaiah 59:19, I stop your evil merchandise in my family in the name of Jesus.

88. I take my blessings by force from the pot, coven and hidden places the witches/wizards have kept them in Jesus' name. (Matt. 11:12.)

89. Standing on Isaiah 8:9, I command every witchcraft association against me to be broken in pieces in Jesus' name.

90. Standing upon Isaiah 8:10a, I command every witchcraft counsel taken against me to come to nought according to the written Word of God in the name of Jesus Christ.

91. In the name of Jesus Christ, I command all words

spoken against me by witches/wizards through any medium to fail and be nullified. (Isaiah 8:10a).

92. In the name of Jesus Christ, I command any hand stretched by witches/wizards to vex me to utterly wither and be consumed by the Holy Ghost fire. (Acts12:1).

93. In the name of Jesus Christ, and standing on Isaiah 6:1, command every witch/wizard standing against the manifestation of my destiny to fall down and die.

94. In the name of Jesus Christ, I command any personality - witch or wizard - placed before me to distract and shield me from receiving divine visitation to be removed right now. (Isaiah 6:1)

95. In the name of Jesus Christ, according to the written judgment of God, every witchcraft horn raised against me, be cut off and be consumed by the Holy Ghost fire. (Psalms 75:10)

96. In the name of Jesus Christ, I command every evil fiood released by witches and wizards in order to overflow me, be dried up right now. (Isaiah 59:19)

97. By the authority in the name of Jesus Christ, I command every witch and wizard assigned to frustrate me in life to be bound and be destroyed by

the Holy Ghost fire.

98. According to Isaiah 14:27a, in the name of Jesus Christ, I command all that the witches and wizards have purposed to achieve in my life to be annulled.

99. According to Isaiah 14:27b, I command every hand of witches and wizards stretched out to execute their evil plans against me to be turned back and be destroyed by the Holy Ghost fire, in the name of Jesus.

100. In the name of Jesus Christ, I command any witchcraft rod stretched towards me to cause havoc in my life to be broken and destroyed by the Holy Ghost fire. (Psalm 125:3)

101. In the name of Jesus Christ, I command the seed of fear planted by witches and wizards in my heart to be uprooted and cast into the Holy Ghost fire. (Mathew 15:13)

102. In the name of Jesus Christ, I command every evil counselor set up against me by witches and wizards to be separated and sent far from me. (Genesis 1:4)

103. According to 1st Corinthians 16:9, in the name of Jesus Christ I command every witch and wizard opposing my great open door of blessings to be bound and be consumed by the Holy Ghost fire.

104. Standing on Gal. 6:8, in the name of Jesus Christ, I uproot every evil seed planted by me through witchcraft manipulations and I cast them into the fire of the Holy Ghost.

105. In the name of Jesus Christ, I command every witchcraft contamination in my life to be destroyed by the blood of Jesus .

106. By the authority in the name of Jesus Christ and the power of the Holy Ghost I revoke every curse that must have come upon me through my past sinful activities.

107. Every witchcraft spirit operating in my family, I command you to be exposed in the mighty name of Jesus Christ.

108. Every household witchcraft spirit operating in my family that sends invitation to outside witches and wizard to torment me and my family, I release the fire of the Holy Ghost against you and your cohorts in the name of Jesus Christ.

109. Every witchcraft deposit located in any part of my body, I release the fire of the Holy Ghost against you and I command you to be expelled from my system in the mighty name of Jesus Christ.

# 3

# STEPS FOR RETAINING DELIVERANCE

# STEPS FOR RETAINING DELIVERANCE

## 1. PUT ON THE WHOLE ARMOUR OF GOD

The Christian's spiritual armour is set forth in Eph. 6:10- 18. There are seven items of this armour:

    **(I) Loins girt about with truth-** Truth is mentioned first among the others because of its importance as the force which holds all the other items together. Truth is the understanding and appreciation of God's revelation of Himself and His accomplished works in the person of Christ. This truth comes through hearing, meditating and believing the Word of God.

    **(ii) The breastplate of righteousness-** Righteousness is a positional state of being free from every sense of guilt and condemnation arising from sin. After you have given your life to Christ, the breastplate of righteousness covers your heart from the fiery darts of negative thoughts and accusations from the devil, who is referred to as "the accuser of brethren" (Rev

12:10). Demons which seek to regain entrance after being cast out of a person assail the mind with negative thoughts. Vehemently resist these demon-inspired thoughts and replace them with positive spiritual thoughts (Phil.4:8) Resist the devil at the first sign of his attack on your mind.

**(iii) Feet shod with the preparation of the gospel of peace-** This armour is very unique and very effective. The "gospel", which means "good news" is the power of God which leads to salvation to them that believe (Romans 1:16). Anyone who actively declares this good news to others, not only releases the power of God to save others, but also for his own protection from the onslaught of satan. Get actively involved in evangelism. (Matt.10:32-33).

**(iv) The shield of faith (Heb.11:6)** Christians have been called to live by faith, not by sight and this distinguishes a believer from an unbeliever (2 Cor. 5:7). Faith is the confident assurance that a person has in God's Word and based on this he/she speaks and acts, not minding contrary circumstances. Your faith is the victory that overcomes the world (1 John 5:4).

**(v) The helmet of salvation-** The helmet is worn on the head and this shows why salvation is symbolized by this armour. Salvation is deliverance from sin and its consequences through the works of Christ on the cross. It is the "head" of every kingdom activity (John 3: 3-5) and opens a believer up to access the benefits of the rest of the armour. Hence you must never compromise your salvation if you must retain your deliverance.

**(vi) The sword of the Spirit which is the Word of God-** This is the only offensive weapon among all the armour. Employing God's Word as a sword is done by declaring same (the Word) to circumstances and situations. Jesus gave us a good example of this in Matthew 4:1-13. The devil came to tempt Him and He employed the "sword" of the spirit by continually declaring "it is written" to him. Putting the Word of God in your mouth is a portent force in spiritual warfare.

**(vii) Praying in the Spirit-** Prayer is spiritual communication between a believer and God through which he receives vital information concerning his faith-walk and protection from the evil plots of satan. However, praying in the Spirit is a higher dimension of this art in which the Holy Spirit takes over the job through the heavenly prayer language known commonly as "speaking in tongues" (Acts 2:1-4). It is very effective in spiritual warfare because it puts the believer above every form of manipulation from satan, as well as building him up in his faith (Romans 8:26-27; Jude 20).

## 2. CONFESS POSITIVELY

Negative confessions characterize demonic influence. Positive confession is faith expressed. Confess what God's Word says. Any contrary confession will open the door for the enemy.

*"For verily I say unto you, That whosoever shall SAY unto this mountain, Be thou removed, and be thou cast into the sea, and shall not doubt in his heart but shall believe that those things which he SAITH shall come to pass, he shall have whatsoever he SAITH"*
*Mark 11:23*

## 3. STAY IN THE SCRIPTURE

Jesus withstood satan's temptation by using Scriptures. The Word is a mirror to the soul (James 1:22-25); it is a lamp unto the feet for guidance (Psalm 119:105); it is a cleansing agent (Eph. 5:25,26); it is a two-edged sword, laying bare the heart (Heb. 4:2); it is food for the spirit (1Peter 2:2; Matt. 4:4). Except the Word of God becomes the primary factor, no person can maintain his or her deliverance for long.

*"Blessed is the man that walketh not in the counsel of the ungodly, nor standeth in the way of sinners, nor sitteth in the seat of the scornful. But his delight is in the law of the Lord; and in his law doth he meditate day and night. And he shall be like a tree planted by the rivers of water that bringeth forth his fruit in his season; his leaf*

*also shall not wither, and whatsoever he doeth shall prosper"Psalm 1:3-5.*

## 4. CRUCIFY THE FLESH

Take your cross daily and follow Jesus (Luke 9:23). Break old habit patterns set up in league with evil spirits. If fleshly appetites, desires and lusts are not brought to the cross, a way for demons to return will be left open (Gal. 5:19-21, 24). To make it easier for you to crucify the flesh, we encourage you to review your old acquaintances with a view to strengthening the relationships which have a godly impact on you. (2Cor.6:16-17)

## 5. DEVELOP A LIFE OF CONTINUOUS PRAISE AND PRAYER

Praise silences the enemy. Praise is an attitude of the heart; it is the expression of adoration, joy and thankfulness unto God, by speaking, singing, shouting, dancing, leaping, playing musical instruments, clapping the hands, etc. Pray in the spirit (in tongues), and also in your understanding (1Cor 14:14). "Pray without ceasing"(1Thes. 5:17).

## 6. MAINTAIN A LIFE OF FELLOWSHIP AND SPIRITUAL MATURITY

It is the sheep that wanders from the flock that is most endangered. Find and fulfill your function within the Body of Christ (church). (See 1Cor. 12:7-14). Keep yourself under spiritual authority.

## 7. COMMIT YOURSELF TOTALLY TO CHRIST

Determine that every thought, word and action will reflect the very nature of Christ. Abide in Christ so that the fruit of the Spirit might come forth in abundance. Demonic spirits are enemies of the fruit of the Spirit. Faith and trust in God are the greatest weapons against the devil's lies.

*"Above all, taking the shield of faith, wherewith ye shall
be able to quench all the fiery dart of the wicked"*
*Eph. 6:16*

**Note:** Doing these seven things will ensure that your"house" (life) is filled after having been cleansed. This way no demon will be able to return or bring any other with him. If a spirit should trick you and regain entrance, see that he is cast out either by yourself or with the help of other believers as soon as you make the observation. If other areas of demonic activities in your life are subsequently brought to light, seek deliverance in those areas too. Do everything possible in line with God's Word to uphold your deliverance on daily basis. Do not settle for anything less!

*"For while we were enemies we were reconciled to God
through the death of His Son, It is much more (certain),
now that we shall be saved (daily delivered from sin's*

*dominion) through His resurrection life." Romans 5:10 Amplified Version.*

## ISSUE OF BLOOD STOPPED

My case was like that of the Biblical woman with the issue of blood. For about 9 years I was experiencing continuous   ow of blood. The case was so bad that I resorted to carrying sanitary pads everywhere I went, even to church. I made several attempts to get help; for many years, I went where ever people suggested the situation could be remedied but the problem de  ed solution.

One day, somebody invited me to attend Voice of Freedom Ministries' Faith clinic. Having suffered much disappointment for a long time, I was reluctant to go but after much persuasion, I reluctantly started attending the clinic. Not long into the prayer program though I felt discouraged and discontinued the follow up sessions.

However, the same person who invited me would not give up on me; she encouraged me to complete the process so I resumed again. This time around as I continued to participate in the ministration, I noticed that the bleeding stopped totally.

Today, I am completely healed and have no need to carry sanitary pads about. I thank the God of VFM!
Sis. Angela I.

## AFFLICTION IN DREAM ENDS
I just want to give thanks to God Almighty for the deliverance He gave to me. For almost five (5), I always see myself eating in my dreams every night. This experience was so frightening that I dreaded sleeping at nights. It got to a time when even in the day time, if I so much as closed my eyes for a nap I would either see myself or someone else eating and when I wake up I would feel the effect of the eating especially in my chest. Apart from the frequent episodes of eating, I usually had sex in my dreams too and I used to experience heat sensations inside my body. While this was happening I would observe myself emaciating and loosing strength for no reason.

I brought these complaints to the Faith Clinic and to the glory of God, there has been tremendous change in my life. I give glory to God for what he has done for me.
**Sis. Vivian E.**

## SPIRIT OF FEAR DESTROYED
For many years I was tormented and afflicted by the spirit of fear. I lived in fear of everything around me, especially darkness. To crown it all, I used to have sex and eat regularly in my dream. There was no type of prayer I did not pray to end this affliction, but the problem remained stubborn and resistant to all my attempts at gaining victory. Then God led me to the Faith Clinic of Voice of Freedom Ministries. After I

went through the teachings followed by the deliverance ministrations I noticed that all the complaints that I came to the clinic with disappeared- the fear, the sex and eating in the dream- all of them stopped! To the glory of God I am now free. **Mrs Victoria A.**

## GOD'S FAVOUR SHOWED UP FOR ME

In March 2012, I came to Benin-city homeless, stranded and confused about life because of numerous problems in my life and family. I had planned to stay with an old time girl friend in town but I was informed that she had traveled overseas long ago. One day along the road, I came across a poster advertising a deliverance program in this church, VFM. I knew that all was not well with my life and I was unhappy so I resolved to attend and participate in the program fully. I went through the Faith Clinic teachings, the deliverance prayers and the prescribed follow up sessions. God proved Himself in my situation; and I began to experience new things in my life. Suddenly, my brother in the U.S remembered me and decided to assist me financially. I was able to start a business which is growing gradually, after a while I secured an accommodation with the help of the same brother. As if that was not enough, I was surprised when he called me one day to say that he was in Nigeria and he bought me a brand new Toyota Camry!

I give all praise to God. I believe in deliverance!
**Sis J. E. J.**

## ANCIENT CURSES BROKEN

I began attending this Faith Clinic due to unpleasant experiences in my dreams. After one of the prayer sessions I had a dream and there was something like a seed on top of my private part which I recognized as the seed of barrenness. I succeeded in pushing it out of me.

In another dream some men had been pursuing me but I turned back and started to pursue them and I killed three of them.

During one of the prayer sessions, the man of God addressed the issue of curses in my life and asked me to come with sand so he can pray with me which I did. That same night in my dream three people confessed that they had used sand against me thus confirming what the man of God prayed about.

One of the days as I prayed with the deliverance book (Effective Deliverance Prayers) at home I saw myself manifesting; I vomited so much. After all these ministrations the yoke is broken and I am now perfectly fine to the glory of God. **Sis. Faith E. O.**

## LOOSED FROM SATANIC BONDAGE

Firstly, before I came to know about this Faith Clinic, I used to experience unexplainable fears- fears I could neither understand nor explain. For example, I used to be terrified of engaging in warfare prayers especially those that had anything to do with praying against witchcraft powers, because during such prayers, I would feel some invisible presence that would attempt to choke me. The fear of going through this experience kept me in bondage and affected my prayer life adversely for a long time. It wasn't until after I went through deliverance ministrations that I was released from this bondage and now I can pray any kind of prayer without any intrusion by dark forces. I was also delivered from the fear of darkness.

Secondly, sometime ago, I began to feel severe pains on my left leg. I did not know why or how the pain started, but one Sunday night 16/04/2017, I had a dream in which I saw somebody put something on the ground for me to step on and thereafter both legs began to swell. In the same dream, I began to pray and I was healed. When I woke up from the dream I discovered that the pain which had been so severe was completely gone. I give God praise for His great deliverance. Thank you, Jesus. **Mrs. Becky A.**

## MULTIPLE STUBBORN ATTACKS QUELLED.

I came here during the program "Freedom 2017". The last Friday of the program was the first day I attended and I came to the program totally discouraged, hopeless and depressed. True, I had a Word of assurance from God to the effect that all would be well but I no longer believed. My entire life was a mess, I did not know what to do or where to go anymore; I had lost all hope in life and in God too. I figured that it would be a relief if my life ended then so I was not really expectant; I just wanted God to take my life.

I had been a Christian for a number of years but then I backslid. In 2007 however, I came to my senses and rededicated my life to Christ- that was when all hell broke loose and my ordeal started. It was on a Sunday after I came back from church, I was sleeping in the afternoon when I had a bad dream. I saw a cousin of mine with a python and she told me that the snake liked me; but I was scared and uncomfortable with it. Before I knew what was happening, the snake gave me a bite on my back and to my surprise, when I woke up, I felt the sting on my back and that was the beginning of my woes.

I was in church one day when I started seeing people that looked like British police coming to attack me with spears, as I continued to pray, things like ants were poured into my private part where they kept moving. I was living in great fear, having bad dreams and eating in the dream. As the attack continued, I started seeing python Leonora coming to attack me (hitting me, moving all over my body, lying on my back, moving round my waist etc). As these attacks were going on, I was moving from place to place, church to church looking for help and deliverance but none was forthcoming instead I grew worse. I began to feel heat sensations under my abdomen, I was seeing hoes and sticks being inserted into my private part, at a time they brought a bucket   lled with tiny snakes and poured into my womb. Strange things would be crawling all over and biting me on my feet, meanwhile, the venom deposited by the serpent on my back kept reacting, giving me the feeling that I was about to suffer a cardiac arrest. I kept vomiting bitter things and some extremely sour, foamy substances. At a point, a serpent would twine itself on my left feet and my left hand attacking and hurting me.

Objects kept moving inside my stomach, and if I dared

conceive, I would be in torment throughout, I would feel hands holding my two legs and pulling them apart as if attempting to tear me into two, then wooden objects would be inserted into my private part to terminate the pregnancy. One time, an invisible hand hit me on my private part between my legs and I suffered a miscarriage.

In an attempt to get my life back, I visited many places, different churches including white garments, mallams (Islamic) witch doctors, but there was no stopping the attacks instead, it kept getting worse.

I started having constant dreams of myself in my village secondary school, no one could tell me what it meant and that was how my finances kept crashing. I moved down from a woman who was having a good life and driven more than 10 cars to the point where I had none. I relocated from Kaduna to join my husband but after the relocation, I found it hard to secure a good job and when I did get one, I never received a complete salary till I left the job at the end of March 2017.

In November 2016, in my dreams, bees and scorpions started stinging me all over my anus, private part and my womb. When I lie down, they come to attack my chest and womb, when I sit; I feel something lifting me, pouring things likes needles/ arrows that hurt like fire into my womb, and private part.

Sometime last year, I had a fire burn attack that affected my private part and my laps and left me with terrible itches that cause injuries, and then I developed inflammatory rashes under my breast.

It was in this state that I came to Voice of Freedom Ministries. I have gone through the Faith Clinic and I stand to testify that I can now see hope where I had been so hopeless and there is light where darkness held sway. God has intervened in the attacks, and I am now pregnant and in peace. I thank God because of His great deliverance and because the devil has lost the battle over my life in Jesus' name. Amen. **Mrs. E. L. F.**

## STOMACH AFFLICTION TERMINATED

For several years, I was afflicted with stomach pain; my stomach for no reason became swollen and painful. Every night the swollen stomach would be shaking and something would be moving inside it. Several visits to hospitals yielded no result.

When I came to the Faith Clinic, I completed the basic ministration procedures and began the follow up ministration. I vomited so many things during this period and surprisingly before the 4th week of the follow up ministration the swelling and accompanying pain was gone. Another testimony is that before I came here, I used to hear a strange voice crying in my ears. Today, I do not hear any strange voice and I am completely free. I give all the glory to God.

# Observations

> *If after or in the course of praying these prayers you observe anything in form of dreams, revelations or any action within your body, ensure to write them in the spaces provided from the next page so you don't forget.*

# OTHER BOOKS BY
## Bishop Abraham
# CHIGBUNDU

- Voice of Freedom (Daily Devotional)
- Loose Him and Let Him Go
- I Believe in Deliverance
- Wicked Times and Seasons
- Witchcraft Manipulations Exposed
- Achievers Secrets
- Developing Another Spirit
- Discover to Recover
- Changing Wicked Times and Seasons'
- From Story to Glory
- Learning in the School of Marriage
- Altar versus Altars
- Spiritual Checkpoint
- Destined for Greatness but Tied
- 30 Secrets of Success
- How to Open Closed Human Destinies
- Overcoming Evil Waters
- Life Transforming Words of Bishop Abraham Chigbundu
- 7 Things God does not Know
- Abiding in His Presence

BREAKING
FAULTY FAMILY
FOUNDATIONS

30
SECRETS
OF
SUCCESS
DR ABRAHAM
CHIGBUNDU

Altars
Deliverance By Sacrific
Dr. Abraham Chigbundu

CHANGING
WICKED
TIMES & SEASONS
DR ABRAHAM
CHIGBUNDU

DESTINED FOR GREATNESS But Tied
A Step-by-step Approach to Securing Your Freedom, Untying Your Destiny, Breaking The Cycle of Delay and Manifesting Greatness
DR ABRAHAM CHIGBUNDU